Walt Disney

ABDO
Publishing Company

Buddy BOOKS
First Biographies

by
Sarah Tieck

VISIT US AT
www.abdopublishing.com

Published by ABDO Publishing Company, 8000 West 78th Street, Edina, Minnesota 55439.

Printed in the United States of America, North Mankato, Minnesota
092009
012010

 PRINTED ON RECYCLED PAPER

Coordinating Series Editor: Rochelle Baltzer
Contributing Editors: Heidi M.D. Elston, Megan M. Gunderson, BreAnn Rumsch, Marcia Zappa
Graphic Design: Jane Halbert
Cover Photograph: *Getty Images*: Alfred Eisenstaedt/Time Life Pictures
Interior Photographs/Illustrations: *AP Photo*: AP Photo (pp. 11, 13, 20, 24), Richard Drew (p. 23), Phelan M. Ebenhack (p. 27), Charlie Riedel (p. 7); *Getty Images*: Alfred Eisenstaedt/Time Life Pictures (p. 16), J.R. Eyerman/Time Life Pictures (p. 29), General Photographic Agency (p. 15), Hulton Archive (pp. 5, 9, 24), Sotheby's/AFP (p. 19).

Library of Congress Cataloging-in-Publication Data

Tieck, Sarah, 1976-
  Walt Disney / Sarah Tieck.
     p. cm. -- (First biographies)
  ISBN 978-1-60453-984-4
  1. Disney, Walt, 1901-1966--Juvenile literature. 2. Animators--United States--Biography--Juvenile literature. I. Title.
  NC1766.U52D585 2010
  791.43092--dc22
  [B]
                              2009031316

Table of Contents

Who Is Walt Disney?

Walt Disney is a famous artist and businessman. His ideas changed the world of cartoons and movies. He won many awards for his work.

Walt is also known for creating Disneyland and Walt Disney World. People still visit these **theme parks** today!

Throughout the years, people around the world have enjoyed Walt's cartoon characters.

Walt's Family

Walter Elias "Walt" Disney was born on December 5, 1901, in Chicago, Illinois. His parents were Flora and Elias Disney. Walt had three brothers and one sister.

When Walt was young, the Disneys moved to a farm in Marceline, Missouri. There, Walt came to love drawing. After a few years, his family moved to Kansas City, Missouri.

Walt always remembered his time in the small town of Marceline.

UNITED STATES

Chicago
Illinois

Marceline
Kansas City

Missouri

Early Life

In 1917, the Disneys returned to Chicago. There, Walt worked to become a better artist. He drew cartoons and took pictures for his high school newspaper. Walt also took classes at the Chicago Academy of Fine Arts.

At this time, the United States was fighting in **World War I**. Walt left school to join the army. But, he was too young to fight. Instead, Walt drove Red Cross **ambulances** in Europe.

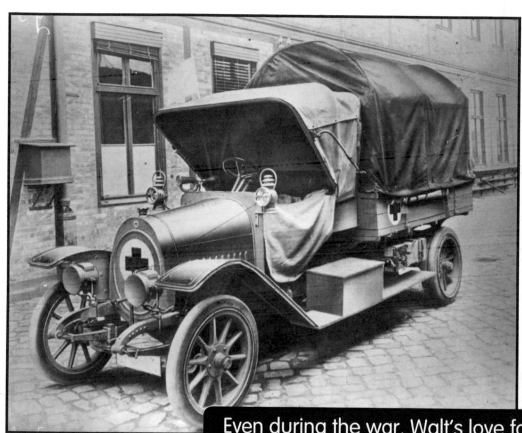

Even during the war, Walt's love for drawing stuck with him. He drew on the sides of Red Cross ambulances!

Starting Out

In 1919, Walt returned to Kansas City. He found work drawing cartoons for **advertisements** in 1920.

In 1923, Walt moved to Los Angeles, California. There, he started the Walt Disney Company with his brother Roy.

UNITED STATES

California

Los Angeles

Walt made short animated cartoons. These movies are created by drawing many pictures. Each picture is a little different from the next. When filmed quickly in a row, the pictures appear to move.

Walt often drew animals for his animated cartoons.

A Growing Family

In 1925, Walt's company hired an artist named Lillian "Lilly" Bounds. Walt and Lilly fell in love. They married that year on July 13.

Later, Walt and Lilly raised a family together. Diane was born in 1933. A few years later, the couple adopted baby Sharon.

As Walt became well known, he traveled the world with his family.

Working Artist

Walt was very interested in improving animation. So, he tried out new ideas. Walt made many short animated cartoons.

Around 1927, Walt created Mickey Mouse. Mickey would become one of the world's most famous cartoon characters!

At first, Walt called his character Mortimer Mouse. But, Lilly thought Mickey was a better name and Walt agreed.

Walt was one of the first animators to add color to his cartoons. And, he made movies that combined cartoons and real people!

In 1928, Walt made a cartoon called *Steamboat Willie*. It stars Mickey Mouse.

At this time, many movies and cartoons were silent. *Steamboat Willie* had sound that went with the pictures. Walt provided the voice of Mickey.

Over the years, Walt made many Mickey Mouse cartoons. He also created characters such as Donald Duck and Pluto.

Award Winner

In 1932, Walt won his first **Academy Award** for *Flowers and Trees*. This cartoon used a new color process. Walt often tried new **technology** to improve his cartoons.

In 1937, *Snow White and the Seven Dwarfs* **debuted**. This was Walt's first full-length feature movie. A lot of work went into creating it. It is considered one of Walt's most important movies.

Snow White and the Seven Dwarfs earned much money for Walt's company. It was one of the top movies of its time.

Walt won four Academy Awards in 1954!

By 1940, Walt's company had made *Pinocchio* and *Fantasia*. These popular movies took much effort to make. So, Walt opened a work space in Burbank, California. He hired more than 1,000 workers!

In Walt's lifetime, his company would create 81 feature films. These include *Bambi*, *Cinderella*, and *Mary Poppins*. Over the years, Walt won more than 25 **Academy Awards**!

Growing a Business

   The Walt Disney Company has grown throughout the years. Walt's talent and efforts helped his company. It became a leader in making cartoons and movies.

   Today, the Walt Disney Company offers people more than just movies. It makes books, television shows, and toys.

Today, the Walt Disney Company makes toys of popular Disney characters.

Walt and his company planned how Disneyland would look.

Sleeping Beauty Castle is a famous part of Disneyland.

One of Walt's most famous ideas was building a **theme park**. He wanted to create a place where families could have fun. Disneyland opened in 1955 in Anaheim, California. It became very popular!

After Disneyland's success, Walt wanted to create bigger parks. In the early 1960s, he began planning Walt Disney World.

An Important Life

Walt did not live to see Walt Disney World completed. He died at age 65 on December 15, 1966. His grave is in Forest Lawn Memorial Park in California.

The Walt Disney Company carried out Walt's work. It completed Walt Disney World, which opened in 1971 in Florida. The company continues to produce movies, cartoons, and television shows.

Pictures and statues of Walt are displayed in his theme parks. There are also books and museum displays about Walt's life.

Today, Walt's lovable animated characters still delight children and adults. His work helped change the way cartoons and movies are made. Walt Disney is remembered as one of the world's greatest creative minds.

Even after Walt's death, his work continued to be honored.

Important Dates

1901 Walt Disney is born on December 5.

1923 Walt and his brother Roy start the Walt Disney Company.

1925 Walt marries Lillian "Lilly" Bounds. They would raise two daughters, Diane and Sharon.

1928 Walt creates the cartoon *Steamboat Willie*, starring Mickey Mouse.

1932 Walt wins his first Academy Award for *Flowers and Trees*.

1937 *Snow White and the Seven Dwarfs* debuts.

1955 Disneyland opens.

1966 Walt Disney dies on December 15.

1971 Walt Disney World opens.

Important Words

Academy Award an award given by the Academy of Motion Picture Arts and Sciences to the best actors and filmmakers of the year.

advertisement (ad-vuhr-TIZE-muhnt) a short message in print or on television or radio that helps sell a product.

ambulance (AM-byuh-luhnts) a vehicle that carries sick or injured people.

debut (DAY-byoo) to make a first appearance.

technology (tehk-NAH-luh-jee) the application of scientific knowledge for practical purposes.

theme park a place with rides, games, and other activities. The buildings and activities are based on one or more central subjects, or themes.

World War I a war fought in Europe from 1914 to 1918.

Web Sites

To learn more about Walt Disney, visit ABDO Publishing Company online. Web sites about Walt Disney are featured on our Book Links page. These links are routinely monitored and updated to provide the most current information available.

www.abdopublishing.com

Index